D1607672

Special Day Prayers
for the
Very Young Child

SPECIAL·DAY PRAYERS

FOR THE VERY YOUNG CHILD

by "Mildred Grenier"
illustrated by Kathy Mitter

CONCORDIA

Several of the poems used in this book were published by Kitchen-Klatter Magazine and used by permission.

Concordia Publishing House, St. Louis, Missouri
Copyright © 1983 Concordia Publishing House

Manufactured in the United States of America

Library of Congress Cataloging in Publication Data

Grenier, Mildred B.
      Special day prayers for the very young child.

      Summary: Contains more than 25 prayers for holidays and special celebrations throughout the year.
      1. Children—Prayer-books and devotions—English.
[1. Prayers] I. Title. BV4870.G76   1983   242'.62
82-14416
ISBN 0-570-04076-0

With love, to Candace and Cheri

WINTER QUEEN

You've blessed me, Lord, this winter day;
I wear my snowflake jewels so bright,
While trees in armor guard my way
I tread a velvet carpet, white.

SHEPHERD OF THE NIGHT

God fills me with love this quiet night
While white sheep clouds are kneeled
And nibble dainty daisy stars
That dot the heaven's clear blue field.

PRAYER FOR FIRST DAY OF WINTER

White snowflakes fall this winter night;
In bed I'm tucked, all snug and tight.
Bless all the people everywhere,
And keep them warm with loving care.

PRAYER FOR CHRISTMAS

On joyful Christmas long ago
You sent a Baby from above
To be the Savior of us all.
I thank You, God, for Your great love.

PRAYER FOR NEW YEAR'S DAY

Dear Father, help me through this year;
Each day, each night, stay very near,
And keep me, in the things I do,
At all times thoughtful, kind, and true.

PRAYER FOR LINCOLN'S BIRTHDAY

He was so honest, Lord,
A friend to all he knew.
Please help me grow to be like him
In everything I do.

PRAYER FOR VALENTINE'S DAY

Thank You, dear Father up above,
For Day of Valentines and love;
On this glad day, and all year through,
I will show love, and kindness too.

PRAYER FOR
GEORGE WASHINGTON'S BIRTHDAY

**Dear Jesus, bless this great man's day,
The Father of Our Country. He
Upheld and loved this land of ours
As my dear Father cares for me.**

WINTER THOUGHTS

Gentle Jesus, bless this winter night;
Against the cold, I'm snug and tight,
While north wind howls and rattles gate—
Then whispers secrets in the grate.

GOODNIGHT

I thank Thee, God, this winter night,
For silently falling snowflakes' flight;
Around earth's icy breast they've spread
A white snow blanket, tucked in tight.

15

SPRING TREASURES

Springtime has come, Lord Jesus—
To winter now, good-bye;
Gold coins were spilled in yard last night
Like pennies from the sky!

HEAVENLY DAY

I'm close to Thee, Lord, this spring day—
I walk in fragrant clouds of rose
While stars of white forget-me-nots
Are twinkling 'round my toes.

PRAYER FOR FIRST DAY OF SPRING

For days of spring, dear Lord, thank You,
For birds and bright rainbow.
Last night the rain danced on the roof;
Today the flowers grow.

PRAYER FOR EASTER

**Thank You for Easter lily's bloom
And that our Savior left the tomb;
For this, to me, does best explain
That I, too, will have life again.**

PRAYER FOR ARBOR DAY

I'm glad, dear God, that we plant trees;
I hear the rustling of their leaves,
In big tree's shade I play and rest,
And in its branches birds build nests.

20

PRAYER FOR MAY DAY

I thank You, Lord, for wind and sun,
For pretty blooms, May basket fun,
For skies of blue, or skies of gray;
I'm glad that I'm alive today!

PRAYER FOR MOTHER'S DAY

I thank You, God, for Mother dear;
My heartfelt thanks for her please hear,
She feeds me, keeps me neat each day,
And helps me, loves me, guides my way.

PRAYER FOR MEMORIAL DAY

I'm thankful that we have this day
To visit graves of loved ones dear;
I place a flower and say a prayer—
They seem so very near.

PRAYER FOR FATHER'S DAY

My father is so good to me
And teaches me so patiently
To work and play, grow strong and tall,
And love You, Father of us all.

PRAYER FOR CHILDREN'S DAY

Bless little children everywhere
God, keep them safe; that is my prayer.
Stay close by them; show them the way
To know and love You, every day.

JUNE PICNIC

I thank Thee, God, for this fair day,
A June parade of sights so gay—
Woodpecker drums, peach trees that spread
Drifts of pink confetti on my head.

PRAYER FOR FIRST DAY OF SUMMER

I love the summertime, dear Lord,
Thank You for this bright day;
The grass is green, bees buzz, birds sing—
Watch o'er them, too, I pray.

27

SUMMER DAWN

I'm grateful, Lord, for summer
When morning paints the dawn
And droplets of her glitter
Drip and glisten on our lawn.

28

SUMMER EVENING

Lord God, I love this summer eve;
When breezes die, the moon comes up—
A shiny, golden penny
Dropped in beggar's blue tin cup.

PRAYER FOR INDEPENDENCE DAY

Thank You for Independence Day;
I'll see parades, the band will play.
Thank You for freedom, sea to sea,
And for the flag that flies for me.

SUMMER STORM

The white bone moon tonight
Hangs by two dangling threads—
A broken button on sky's black coat,
Which storm has left in shreds.

SUMMER JOY

This bright day fills my heart with joy—
Jets' white chalk marks so high
Play tic-tac-toe on brilliant
Blue bulletin boards in the sky.

PRAYER FOR FIRST DAY OF SCHOOL

Warm months of summer now are past;
September days are here at last.
I'll do my best at work and play
At school, for it begins today.

PRAYER FOR LABOR DAY

For Labor Day, dear Lord, I'm glad,
For we must work, like Mom and Dad.
Help me each day to do my share
And not complain. This is my prayer.

PRAYER FOR FIRST DAY OF FALL

Lord God, I'm thankful for the fall;
You've planned for everything.
The leaves will fall and plants will sleep,
But all will grow next spring.

AUTUMN PICTURES

My heart is joyous, sweet Jesus—
Leaves hop and skip, play running games;
Like candles, all fence posts are lit
With scarlet ivy flames.

AUTUMN PRAYER

Jesus, this autumn time of year
Bless flying birds and wildlife, please;
While rustling leaves and dried corn stalks
Whisper "October" in the breeze.

PRAYER FOR FRIEND'S BIRTHDAY

Thank You, dear Lord, for my good friend,
Whose birthday is today.
I'm thankful, God, I have this friend
Who shares my work and play.

PRAYER FOR MY BIRTHDAY

I thank You, God, for this glad day—
I feel so close to You.
Now each day in the year to come
Guide me in all I do.

PRAYER FOR COLUMBUS DAY

This day is named for one so brave
Who guided ships through ocean's wave
And found America so grand;
I'm glad I live in this great land.

PRAYER FOR PARENTS' ANNIVERSARY

I'm thankful, Lord, for Mom and Dad,
Who married and had me.
Please bless them on this special day:
Their anniversary.

PRAYER FOR HALLOWEEN

At Halloween it's so much fun;
I wear a mask and laugh and run.
But I'll not scare a little tot,
Or play a prank that I should not.

PRAYER FOR A BIRTH

For this sweet baby that You sent
To us on this glad day,
Lord, help me show my love and care
In all I do and say.

PRAYER FOR GRANDPARENTS' DAY

For dear and sweet grandparents, God,
I'm thankful every day;
They laugh and walk and play with me—
Please watch o'er them, I pray.

PRAYER FOR A WEDDING

God, bless this woman and this man
Who stand before You here
And help them make a happy home
Filled with Your love and cheer.

PRAYER FOR VETERAN'S DAY

Dear Father, bless each family
Of those who died for You and me,
They bravely fought on land and sea
And gave their lives to keep us free.

PRAYER FOR THANKSGIVING DAY

For eyes to see, and ears to hear
The voices of my family dear,
For arms and legs to run and play,
I thank You, God, each hour, each day.

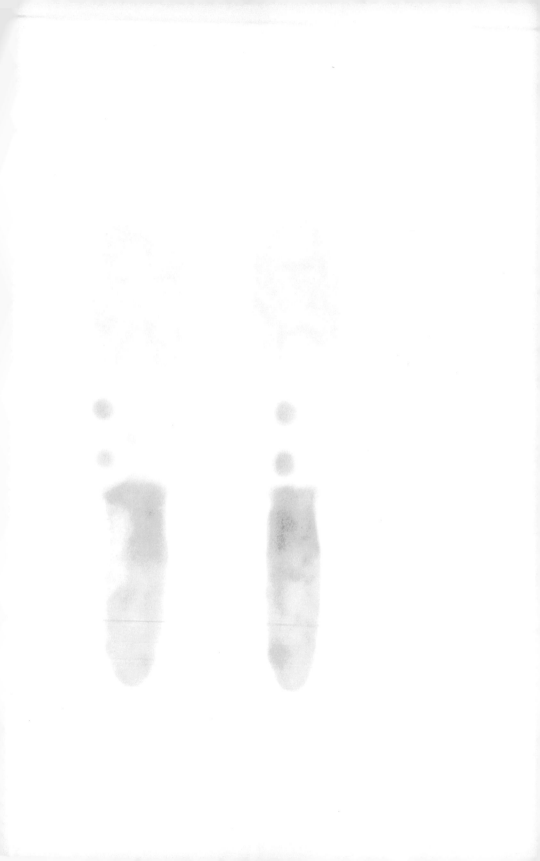